The Zoomorphic Mask

Nicholas Penny
Thaw Senior Fellow 2018

DRAWING INSTITUTE
THE MORGAN LIBRARY & MUSEUM

Nicholas Penny

The Zoomorphic Mask

The Annual Thaw Lecture 2018

DRAWING INSTITUTE
THE MORGAN LIBRARY & MUSEUM

DNE AD ADIVVAV
ME FE   STINA

Foreword

The Morgan's Drawing Institute, founded in 2011 with an endowment gift from Eugene V. Thaw, is now eight years old. While the program continues to grow, it has also established a regular annual sequence of lectures, graduate seminars and masterclasses, occasional publications, predoctoral and postdoctoral fellows, and—every spring—a Senior Fellow, who works on a project of his or her choosing, who teaches a graduate seminar and masterclass, and who delivers the Annual Thaw Lecture. In choosing our Senior Fellow, we look to scholars of great standing, but not only at those focused on drawings alone. Instead, we hope to find someone who will offer new perspectives on drawing.

The 2018 Thaw Senior Fellow, Sir Nicholas Penny, does precisely this in the present publication, our fourth volume in the series of Annual Thaw Lectures. When he began his career as Keeper of Western Art at the Ashmolean Museum in Oxford, the superb drawing collection there fell under his purview, but Nick went on to be Curator of Renaissance Painting at the National Gallery in London, from 1990 to 2000, and then Senior Curator of Sculpture at the National Gallery of Art in Washington from 2002 to 2008, before he returned to London to serve as Director of the National Gallery from 2008 to 2015. The range of Nick's publications is impressive, running from catalogues of European sculpture at the Ashmolean, to his studies of picture frames, to his indispensable catalogues of the sixteenth-century Italian paintings at the National Gallery. His monograph on Raphael, written with Roger Jones back in 1983, remains the best general study of the artist, and his *Taste and the Antique: The Lure of Classical Sculpture*, written with Francis Haskell in 1981, has been through at least seven different printings and revised editions, perhaps the rarest accomplishment imaginable for an academic monograph. It was a great pleasure to have him at the Morgan Drawing Institute, for he could be relied on to make an interesting comment about virtually every work that appeared in our study room.

As he makes clear in the pages that follow, drawings and prints of grotesque ornament both reflected the work of painters and sculptors and also stimulated them, and encouraged the transfer of ideas from one medium to another. This gives the topic a special appeal for an author who has long divided his research between the various arts. His lecture explores some of the most celebrated works of art in New York—the Morgan's *Farnese Hours* and the splendid portrait by Bronzino at the Metropolitan Museum of Art—but connects them with little-known drawings and prints and also with some of Manhattan's early twentieth-century architecture. Similarly, he turns here to Michelangelo, but looks at some of the least-studied aspects of that great master's art: the grotesque masks that are overlooked partly because they are not necessarily carved by him and partly because they are not quite what is studied under the heading of architecture. As Nick makes clear, however, drawing remained the medium in which these ideas from ancient art were studied and redesigned so that they could be carried forward into new painting, sculpture, and architecture, from the Renaissance to the present.

As always, in addition to offering my appreciation to the author of the Annual Lecture, I must acknowledge the role played by the members of the Department of Drawings and Prints—in 2018, John Marciari, Jennifer Tonkovich, Austėja Mackelaitė, Marco Simone Bolzoni, Zoe Watnik, and Alexandra Coutavas—in so generously hosting our fellows, and in bringing the Annual Lectures to publication.

Colin B. Bailey
Director, The Morgan Library & Museum

Nicholas Penny

The Zoomorphic Mask

Clovio's Masks

By 1546, when Giulio Clovio (1498–1578) completed work on his master-
piece, the *Farnese Hours*, the margins of devotional books had long been
adorned with precious stones, ancient cameos, flowers, animals, and monsters. For Cardinal Alessandro Farnese (1520–1589), who was a very young
man when he commissioned this work, Clovio added to such distractions
panoramic landscapes and an unprecedented number of nude figures, the
majority of them female. He lavished as much care and imagination on the
fictive frames that are populated by these nudes as he did on the sacred narratives they surround. For any commentator the question must always be
whether or to what extent these frames should be considered as "merely"
ornamental.[1]

For his depiction of the Visitation and the allegorical scene on the fac- FIG 1
ing page, Clovio supplied a fictive frame of unpatinated bronze incorporat-
ing half-nude female figures, some of them tethering unicorns (emblems
of purity), but others merely serving as the elegant supporters of tablets
adorned with cameos.[2] The larger cameos allude to other episodes in the
life of the Virgin Mary, so these, too, even more obviously than the unicorns, are relevant to the sacred subject.

1 Giulio Clovio
The Visitation and *The Embrace of Justice and Peace* ca. 1540

The Morgan Library & Museum,
New York

Clovio frequently allowed the figures in the frames to come to life and to match in size the figures in the narratives, which enabled him to establish witty relationships between them. Thus, the nude youths supporting swags in the upper part of the frame around the *Annunciation to the Shepherds* (figures that were obviously derived from Michelangelo's Sistine Chapel ceiling) look as if they are rehearsing for the acrobatic pose of one of the nude shepherds, while the elegant nude female on the left side of the frame, around whom a purple scarf swirls, and still more the putto above with split legs, seem to mimic the angel in the sky.[3] In such instances the nude framing figures might even be suspected of deliberately subverting the seriousness of the narratives.

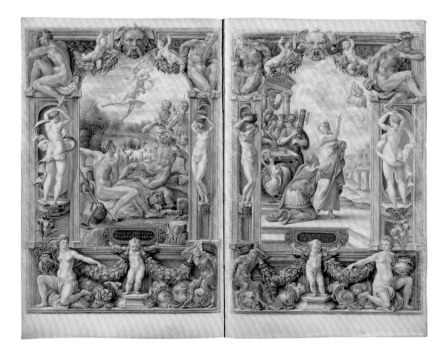

2 Giulio Clovio
*The Annunciation to the
Shepherds* and *The Prophecy of the
Tiburtine Sibyl* ca. 1540

The Morgan Library & Museum,
New York

The nude women on either side of King David, their bodies turned toward him as he kneels in penance, seem almost to be in the same room FIG 3 as he is—and elements of the frame echo the furniture of his private oratory.[4] These figures may embody the libidinous thoughts that the king fails to repress, or at least refer to his adulterous passion for Bathsheba.[5] That this is the case gains strong support from the fact that the youths on the opposite page bear the head of Goliath and the shepherd boy's sling, in allusion to the young David's heroic deeds, contrasted with the shameful one depicted in the frame, where Bathsheba's husband is slaughtered.

Ignudi, the ornamental nudes that became so popular in sixteenth-century Italian and Italianate art, like the putti who accompany them, generally have no specific identity or obvious meaning, even if they sometimes

3 Giulio Clovio
The Death of Uriah and *David in Penance* ca. 1545

The Morgan Library & Museum, New York

assume an allegorical purpose and occasionally, as here, suggest a possible extension to the narrative. This is surely also true of the masks that abound in Clovio's frames. There are more than seventy of them, if we include the half dozen in the silver-gilt binding made for the book by Antonio Gentili in the early seventeenth century, but their variety will here be illustrated in a few examples. The first can be found in the frame for the *Visitation* and is one of a group of four masks, if we include the matching frame on the opposite page. On close examination, they are all different, but this one has grown the tentacles of an octopus.[6] The second example is a prominent feature of the frame surrounding the *Annunciation to the Shepherds*, and the other examples are profile masks from the frame of *David in Penance*.

FIG 4

FIG 5

FIGS 6A, 6B

4   Giulio Clovio
    Detail of fig. 1

5   Giulio Clovio
    Detail of fig. 2

6A, 6B   Giulio Clovio
         Details of fig. 3

Clovio's masks, all of which seem to be male, are only partly human and are always ugly, unlike the female masks which, together with cherubim, appear on the book's silver-gilt cover and are beautiful, with radiant if somewhat blank expressions.[7] In common with the female masks, however, Clovio's masks are often crowned with a diadem and framed below, from ear to ear, by a swag of drapery resembling a napkin or a bib, modified in one of the examples here as a gag. Their hair and beards have sometimes turned into foliage. Their ears are often oversized, and some have dewlaps, many have sprouted wings or horns, and one (as noted) has grown tentacles. In addition to being partially vegetal or animal, the majority of them are mineral—that is, fictive sculptures of metal or stone. Those which are large and flesh-colored, as in the second and third examples here, seem likely to have most significance, but what that might be is not easy to guess, especially in the case of the second and largest example. Most of the masks seem unhappy as well as ugly. Occasionally, there is something like an inane grin, as in the first example, or a hint of malicious merriment, but more commonly their features are distorted by anger or sorrow or suffering. The expressions of the masks around the *Death of Uriah* and *David in Penance* are especially agonized and surely respond to the painful nature of the subject.

This essay traces the origin of such masks and provides a sketch of their history, before and after Clovio, in sculpture, painting, and architecture, touching on their significance and meaning, inasmuch as that can be deduced. Special attention is given to Michelangelo, for whom such masks had an importance that has seldom been acknowledged.

Grotesque Ornament

Clovio, regarded as the greatest miniaturist of his day, was close to Michelangelo, and his exact copies of some of the most finished drawings by that artist are well known. There is also plenty of evidence that he was familiar with the paintings of Raphael, and he was certainly greatly influenced by the work of Raphael's associate and protégé Giovanni da Udine (1487–1564). Both Clovio and Giovanni had been in the service of Cardinal Marino Grimani during the 1530s, although Giovanni's most celebrated work had been executed earlier in the century and was to be seen on the second floor of the Vatican Palace. This was the Loggia of Pope Leo X, a vaulted corridor

7　Giovanni da Udine
**Ornamental fresco in the Loggia
of Pope Leo X** 1518–19

The Vatican Palace, Vatican City

with a succession of arches, originally open to the sky, where a series of sacred narratives, commonly known as "Raphael's Bible" and painted by his assistants, were surrounded by profane ornament devised by Giovanni da Udine and executed both in low-relief stucco and in fresco.[8] It provides a parallel, on a much larger scale, for the combination of the edifying and the entertaining that is to be found in Clovio's illuminated books.

Giovanni da Udine's work in stucco and fresco in the Loggia in 1518–19 FIG 7 was a revival, in both style and technique, of the decoration in the subterranean ruins not far from the Colosseum, grottoes we now know to have been part of the Domus Aurea, the Golden House of Nero.[9] Such ornaments were known as *grottesche*, a term in use in Italy as early as 1502,[10] here translated as "grotesques," although in sixteenth- and seventeenth-century English "antic work" was preferred. Grotesques were a sort of "divertimento" or "light entertainment—a kind of pictorial quodlibet," which also embodied "a manifestation of artistic freedom, paradoxically but correctly claiming legitimacy for . . . absurdities in what was anti-classical in antique art."[11] Such ornament was characterized as anticlassical because Vitruvius, the ancient authority on what was correct or canonical, had explicitly condemned it. It also included hybrid monsters of the kind ridiculed by Horace, one of the most admired of ancient poets.[12] The question of freedom or licence is one to which we will return.

For Clovio, as also for Giorgio Vasari, Giovanni da Udine's grotesques were associated not only with Raphael but with Michelangelo. Indeed, perhaps because he found working with Giulio Romano to be difficult, Giovanni seems to have offered his services to Michelangelo very soon after Raphael's death.[13] Having decorated a room in the Medici palace by 1523, he agreed to execute stucco ornament for the coffered dome of Michelangelo's New Sacristy (a Medici funerary chapel) for San Lorenzo in Florence, work that was eventually undertaken in October 1532 but was suspended in the following year.[14] No trace or even record has survived of the "foliage, birds, masks and figures" that had been so admired by Vasari. Nor do we even know why this work was removed in the 1750s.[15]

Other artists before Giovanni da Udine had studied the subterranean Roman ruins by torchlight. Pinturicchio imitated the painted ornaments that he found there in the 1490s and thereafter in other locations, most notably the Piccolomini Library in Siena Cathedral, where work began in 1503.[16] The black background, the slender tendril supports, the satyrs and putti, also the foliate masks he employed, all derived from Roman mural painting, where, however, the decorative schemes are never as crowded and busy. Pinturicchio (ca. 1452–1513)—or perhaps a specialist assistant of his named Bimbo[17]—found a creature with an elongated neck and tail especially useful for filling awkward spaces. Such creatures make a memorable appearance on the maiolica tiles supplied by Pinturicchio for Pandolfo

FIG 8

Petrucci's Sienese palace in 1509.[18] Although they do have something in common with the miniature bristling harpies in Roman mural decoration, their polymorphic elasticity suggests a different ancestry.[19]

A drawing in the Morgan Library & Museum that appears to date from the same period—that is, from about 1510—shows two halves of a pilaster panel filled with a candelabrum of grotesque ornament, probably intended

FIG 9

to be carved, or painted in imitation of carving.[20] The most substantial hybrid here, combining a female head and torso with wings and lion's legs, is a sphinx that must be derived from ancient Roman sculpture. The other

8   Associate of Pinturicchio
Floor tile from the Petrucci Palace, Siena 1509

Tin-glazed earthenware
Private collection

monsters, especially those on the right side of the sheet, intended for the upper part of the pilaster, may have been derived from northern European sources. They recall the demons torturing Saint Anthony in Martin Schongauer's much-admired engraving,[21] which Domenico Ghirlandaio urged the young Michelangelo to copy and color.[22] Creatures of this kind, combined with antique Roman motifs, were to flourish throughout the following century.

FIG 10

Further evidence of the way that monsters from north of the Alps mingled with motifs from the Golden House of Nero can be found in a group of drawings by Cesare da Sesto (1497–1523), which he must have made in Rome, also about 1510.[23] Cesare's studies after frescoes by Raphael and Michelangelo are mingled with monsters and monstrous ornament. On one sheet we find a nude figure balanced on a slender scroll. Beneath the figure, there is an animal's head with inverted ram's horns and long mustaches. At the bottom of the sheet, there is a creature with human legs, a proboscis, and a foliate tail.[24] The first of these must have been suggested by ancient Roman ornament, the second may have been, but the third has clearly strayed from the world of Schongauer or Hieronymus Bosch. In another drawing by Cesare we find a foliate eagle's head and above that a monstrous head composed of two heads in profile. Wings grow out of the top of these heads, whiskers sweep away beneath, and, between wings and whiskers, there issue the legs of a crab.[25] The idea of the composite

FIG 11

FIG 12

9 Unknown Italian artist
   **Design for a relief of a grotesque
   candelabrum intended to fill a
   pilaster relief (in two parts, the
   lower to the left)** ca. 1510

   The Morgan Library & Museum,
   New York

10 Probably Michelangelo
Buonarotti after the engraving
by Martin Schongauer
*The Torment of Saint
Anthony* ca. 1487

Kimbell Art Museum,
Fort Worth

11 Cesare da Sesto
**Sheet from a Roman sketchbook,
with two studies of female
nudes, Leda and the Swan,
the Infant Christ and Infant
Saint John with several
grotesques** ca. 1508–13

The Morgan Library & Museum,
New York

12 Cesare da Sesto
    **Sheet from a Roman sketchbook,
    with studies of Judith with
    the Head of Holofernes, David
    with the Head of Goliath,
    the Virgin and Child, and
    grotesques** ca. 1508–13

    The Morgan Library & Museum,
    New York

13 Unknown artist
Gradual of Pope Leo X, featuring the letter O ca. 1519

The Morgan Library & Museum, New York

14 Severo Calzetta da Ravenna
Marine Monster ca. 1500–1510

The Metropolitan Museum of Art, New York

head, which centuries later was to become a major theme in the paintings of Pablo Picasso, had its source in medieval ornament and is found in a spectacular illuminated manuscript made for Pope Leo X in Rome in the same period.[26] In this case the profile heads that flank the initial O are of a FIG 13 medieval type known as the Green Man.

Roman mural decorations commonly featured masks, sometimes the head of Medusa (gorgoneion), sometimes theatrical masks, sometimes personifications of the ocean; some of these last survive today in the ruins of the Golden House. Such a marine association must explain why Severo Calzetta da Ravenna (active by 1496) considered them suitable for his sea monsters.[27] Although these antique examples were certainly a source for both FIG 14 Pinturicchio and Giovanni da Udine and their contemporaries, there must also have been some knowledge of the Green Man type of mask, which had been a popular ornament in stone and wood carving for centuries north of the Alps and is also found in manuscript illumination at an even earlier date.[28] In them (as can be seen in fig. 13) not only do the beard and hair but also the cheeks turn into leaves, and branches sometimes issue from the mouth or sprout from the ears. Such foliate masks enjoyed great popularity in early sixteenth-century ornament prints, whereby they spread to all parts of Europe.[29] They became more fantastic and are sometimes also so completely foliate as to escape the notice of the casual viewer.[30] They might also include the horns and ears of sheep or goats, the wings of birds or bats, or the fins of fish, and they evolved into the variety of hybrid masks which are to be found in the *Farnese Hours*.

Michelangelo's Designs for Grotesque Ornament

The greatest European artist to concern himself with inventions of this kind was Michelangelo. The earliest of his surviving drawings which reflect this interest in grotesque ornament seem to date from about 1504, not long before he is likely to have designed the frame for the *Doni Tondo*. What distinguishes these designs is a concern to bend ornament into a semi-abstract order, for which reason he perhaps preferred the concentrated symmetry of a capital to the loosely assembled candelabrum filling a pilaster. Even in a continuous frieze such as that of the *Doni Tondo* frame, he established tight sculptural units (we might even describe them as stanzas), repeated with variations, rather than flowing motifs. The two monsters in a drawing in the British Museum, with their bodies facing inward and necks entwined so that they face the scrolling tails, are very similar to those in the *Doni Tondo*

FIG 15

15 Michelangelo Buonarotti
Studies for grotesque capitals,
with a separate mask and lines
from a sonnet ca. 1504(?)

The British Museum, London

16 Probably designed by
Michelangelo Buonarotti, perhaps
carved by Domenico del Tasso
Detail of the frame of
Michelangelo's *Doni*
Tondo ca. 1504(?)

Gallerie degli Uffizi, Florence

frame, which are centered on a foliate mask.[31] Turning the sheet, we find a
more complex design, also for a capital, in which foliate masks and serpen-
tine birds are involved.[32] Caroline Elam has pointed out that these designs
for capitals (the purpose of which is unknown) have much in common with
the capitals created a decade earlier by Giuliano da Sangallo for the sacristy
of Santo Spirito in Florence.[33] They are also the prelude to the astonishing
inventions that Michelangelo made for the New Sacristy of San Lorenzo a
decade later.

For the New Sacristy, Michelangelo devised a new type of composite
capital to crown the paired fluted pilasters.[34] Acanthus is replaced with
fluted shells which echo the curves of the masks, and the volutes are
adapted to suggest projecting horns. Fragmentary ancient capitals may
have inspired these,[35] but no two masks are the same, thus preserving the
rich variety of invention within the apparent symmetry—rhyme, as it were,
replacing repetition as the ordering agent. Even more extraordinary is the
frieze of highly stylized masks with darts that Michelangelo devised for the
walls.[36] Such an invention, derived from the egg-and-dart motif of ancient
Greek origin, could only have been made by someone who had reflected on

FIG 16

FIG 17

FIG 18

17 Designed by Michelangelo
Buonarotti, perhaps carved by
Francesco da Sangallo
Pilaster capitals ca. 1524

The New Sacristy, San Lorenzo,
Florence

18 Designed by Michelangelo
Buonarotti, perhaps carved by
Francesco da Sangallo
Frieze of masks and darts
ca. 1524

The New Sacristy, San Lorenzo,
Florence

the process of abstraction in the origin of ornament. Yet more grotesque masks can be found on the sides of the miniature vases that adorn the blind windows of the walls. They also feature on the figural sculpture.

In designing the two effigies of the Medici dukes for the New Sacristy, Michelangelo would have recalled that in antique Roman sculpture the helmet or headdress often took the form of an animal's head, usually that of a lion, and the head of Medusa often appeared on the cuirass worn by military commanders. He surely also remembered Verrocchio's profile bust reliefs of Alexander and Darius in which the ferocity of the human hero is projected through fantastic ornaments on head and chest armor. More specifically, he took up an idea that Giuliano da Sangallo had played with in his Sienese sketchbook, that of applying masks from grotesque ornament for this same purpose.[37] The mask on Giuliano de' Medici's chest is so expressive and prominent that it makes a stronger impression on the viewer than do the features of the duke's own face.[38] Michelangelo seems to have had little sympathy for plants (or, indeed, for landscape), and the projections that were often foliate in earlier grotesque masks, including those in his own drawings, are here converted into cartilaginous whiskers,

FIG 19

19 Michelangelo Buonarotti
Duke Giuliano de' Medici carved
ca. 1531–33 and abandoned,
unfinished, in 1534

The New Sacristy, San Lorenzo,
Florence

spines, fins, or wings.[39] There are additional small masks on the buckles of
the shoulder straps attaching Giuliano's cuirass. And the personification of
Night nearby also has a mask by her side, beyond which we see the "mask-
and-dart" frieze (see fig. 29).

In the case of the effigy of Lorenzo, the grotesque mask may at first seem
less obvious, but the wolflike snout with long ears beside it has as its crest
a concave hollow with vertical divisions.[40] This motif, which in the ear-

FIG 20

lier discussion of Clovio's masks was described as a diadem, has a quasi-
architectural character and certainly derives from ornamental masks of
ancient Rome, where the form was borrowed from the tiles on ancient
Etruscan roofs.[41] Lorenzo also rests his elbow on a mysterious casket, the
front of which is adorned with the startled face of a bat-like creature with
large ears.

20 Michelangelo Buonarotti
Duke Lorenzo de' Medici carved
ca. 1533–34 and abandoned,
unfinished, in 1534

The New Sacristy, San Lorenzo,
Florence

One other ornament in the New Sacristy should be mentioned here: the long, ribbon-like serpents above the segmental pediments of the empty niches beside Giuliano. These seem to have been developed from the wriggling polymorphic creatures in the *Doni Tondo* frame. Similar creatures appear in the rectangular panels at the base of the candelabrum on the altar.[42] We know that Michelangelo did not carve the architectural ornament in the chapel. Much of it, including the candelabrum, was the work of the sculptor in whom he placed most confidence, Silvio Cosini (1495–ca. 1549),[43] who incorporated this type of ornament into work of his own design. The influence of Cosini can be seen in the marble altar frame now

FIG 21 serving as a doorway in the Blumenthal Patio in the Metropolitan Museum of Art, New York, where very similar creatures nestle within rectangular panels.[44] Included in the same album as the drawings by Cesare da Sesto is a fine black-chalk study of a rather unhappy monster, which must be

FIG 22 preparatory for a relief of this kind.[45]

An idea of the evolution of Michelangelo's designs for grotesque ornament can be obtained by comparing two of the four panels on the front

21 In the style of Silvio Cosini
    **Detail of altar frame now serving
    as a doorway in the Blumenthal
    Patio** ca. 1535–40

    The Metropolitan Museum of
    Art, New York

22 Italian artist close to Michelangelo
    (previously attributed to Camillo
    Boccaccino)
    **Study for an architectural compartment
    containing a relief of a monster with
    coiled tail and web feet** ca. 1530

    The Morgan Library & Museum,
    New York

23 Probably designed by
    Michelangelo Buonarotti
    Panel of grotesque ornament
    from the tomb of Pope
    Julius II ca. 1510

    San Pietro in Vincoli, Rome

24 Probably designed by
    Michelangelo Buonarotti
    Panel of grotesque ornament
    from tomb of Pope
    Julius II ca. 1533

    San Pietro in Vincoli, Rome

of the lowest stage of the tomb of Pope Julius II in San Pietro in Vincoli.
One was surely made, or at least designed, when Michelangelo first began
FIG 23 work on this commission, in about 1510 if not earlier, and the other perhaps
FIG 24 more than two decades later, after he had designed the low-relief serpents
mentioned above for the New Sacristy.[46] The earlier panel may seem somewhat conventional, although the elegance of line, the balance of figure and
ground, the rhymes between wings and leafy beards, the fluent metamorphosis as profile foliate masks turn into fronds that curl up to form a horn
of plenty are remarkable enough. In the later panel, however, there is an
extraordinary originality both in the rhyming and metamorphosis and in
the sweeping lines of low relief that suggest not only a certain type of wash
drawing combined with the calligraphic ink-line drawn with a quill but
also an interest in emulating the way that stucco can be manipulated with
a spatula when it is still soft.[47] The images seem to have been derived from
the line. However original in style, the motifs were not entirely new. Where
we expect to find heads in the top left and right corners, there are buds or
snails such as may also be found in place of heads in the grotesque design
for a pilaster discussed above (see fig. 9). As a style of carving, the only prec-
edent that comes to mind is Pietro Lorenzetti's spout in the bathroom of

Cardinal Bernardo Bibbiena, decorated, significantly, with grotesques by Giovanni da Udine.[48] Designs of this kind must have been known to Alessandro Allori, who adopted the same motifs in his ceiling frescoes in the corridor of the Uffizi in 1581.[49]

"Signor Michael" Defends the Grotesque

The Portuguese miniature artist Francisco De Hollanda was in Rome in 1538 or 1539. In addition to possessing a keen interest in Roman antiquity,[50] he knew and greatly admired the work of Giulio Clovio, to whom he refers as Don Giulio of Macedonia. Clovio must at that date have just begun work on the *Farnese Hours*, which he was to complete only in 1546. De Hollanda mentions Michelangelo's admiration for Clovio, which is documented by other sources. On his return to Portugal in 1540, De Hollanda wrote his treatise on ancient painting, attaching to it dialogues in which both Clovio and Michelangelo play a part. The finished work is dated 1548, although he may have drafted much of it considerably earlier.[51] A large part of the dialogues concerns grotesque ornament.

"And now, Signor Michael, said Zapata the Spaniard . . . I cannot understand . . . why is it a common practice to paint—as we see in many parts of this city—a thousand monsters and beasts some with the faces of women and the tails of fish, others with the legs of tigers and with wings." Michelangelo's reply is not easy to follow. He begins by showing himself to be aware of Horace's condemnation of capricious hybrids in *Arts poetica* but argues that imaginative freedom is validated when creatures of fancy do not look ridiculous or like mistakes but possess a certain plausibility. He cites stags that are also fish, figures with wings in place of arms, putti emerging from buds, tabernacles made of reeds—examples that show he was also aware of the condemnation of such ornamental motifs by Vitruvius, though the latter is not mentioned here by name.[52] Michelangelo also observes that the deployment of grotesque ornament is not always appropriate, and De Hollanda himself makes a puzzling reference to the subject of the Penitence of King David, in which there may perhaps be an echo of a controversy surrounding Clovio's depiction of this very rare subject (see fig. 3).[53]

One of the best recent scholarly accounts of De Hollanda considers it to be unlikely that such opinions were "acquired . . . directly from

Michelangelo, who employed this type of decoration very sparingly in his own work."[54] But, if it is accepted that Michelangelo designed the ornament in the New Sacristy and for the tomb of Julius II, and if we also recall Michelangelo's admiration for Giovanni da Udine and for Clovio, also his designs for metalwork,[55] then it is very likely that he had opinions on this subject. Furthermore, given that the ornamental reliefs were designed by Michelangelo himself but not executed by him, it makes more sense that elsewhere in the dialogues he should explain that marble carving was a sort of painting and that work on paper should have priority over work with the chisel.[56]

The reliability of De Hollanda's dialogues will always be controversial, but David Summers was surely correct to argue that they do indeed reveal some of Michelangelo ideas,[57] and the way that the argument seems so obviously scrambled, as if partially lost in recollection, transcription, or translation, supports this, for something freely invented would have been far more coherent and fluent.

Michelangelo's Later Architectural Masks

Studies of Michelangelo's sculpture seldom mention the grotesque ornament or his designs for goldsmiths, doubtless because they confine themselves to works that he modeled or carved himself. It may also be assumed that ornament belongs to his work as an architect. Studies of his architecture likewise neglect such ornaments because they are now thought of as marginal.[58] But they may provide us with a valuable insight. As he came to endow separate elements of architecture—capitals, pediments, corbels, and even base moldings—with a novel freedom or license, so he also linked some of them with fantastic creatures, obvious manifestations of anti-Vitruvian *invenzione*.[59] Thus, on the convex abacus above the moldings that serve as capitals for the slim Doric columns which nestle in pairs in the vestibule of the Laurentian Library, we find bat-like masks, one with horns,

FIG 25 the other with large ears.[60]

These prepare us for the new style of Ionic capital that he invented for the Palazzo dei Conservatori on the Capitoline Hill in Rome—one of his most influential creations.[61] In these, volutes of unprecedented elasticity are coiled below grotesque masks which themselves feature similarly curl-

FIG 26 ing, leathery extensions.[62] And then, after creating a whole frieze of masks

25 Designed by Michelangelo
Buonarotti
**Capitals of the Doric
columns** 1523–26

Staircase vestibule of the
Laurentian Library, San
Lorenzo, Florence

26 Designed by Michelangelo
Buonarotti
Ionic capital ca. 1563

Palazzo dei Conservatori, Rome

in the courtyard of the Palazzo Farnese, also in Rome, Michelangelo devised the largest of all his masks to crown the keystone of the great arched opening of his final work of architecture, the Porta Pia in that same city.[63] This mask is the last sculpture that he made—if we allow into this category works that he designed and the execution of which he probably supervised.[64] The mask (or, more likely, one of his drawings for it) was engraved soon after he died,[65] and its influence suggests that his contemporaries gave it more attention than have modern scholars. A spectacular drawing by the Cavalier d'Arpino (1568–1640) shows the mask given life and color, and the stylized coiling of the beard transferred to the hair.[66]

FIG 27

FIG 28

The Porta Pia mask rises from the keystone (which is also a volute) like a bust on a pedestal. Its diadem is now integrated with the architectural forms around it, in both its concavity and its segmental outline. The giant ears are turned outside in and curled, as if aspiring to be volutes. The bulging brows, which are almost as prominent as the nose, twist upward to meet these ears, reversing the downward curvature of the massive mustache. This mustache is placed in front of the beard, in which on each side there are deep and regularly spaced divisions. The monumentality of this

33

27 Designed by Michelangelo
Buonarotti between 1561 and
1564 and carved probably by
Giacomo del Duca
**Mask above the keystone of the
principal arch** 1568

Porta Pia, Rome

mask depends not only on such bold and almost geometric simplifications
but on the shadows created by the deep cavities of mouth, eyes, and ears.

Colleagues in other branches of art history have had no difficulty in
assigning identities to masks in Chinese tombs, Indonesian temples, or Japanese armor, but Michelangelo's masks have attracted little exegesis, even
of a parenthetical and tentative nature. There is nothing in the literature
of his time that helps, except for the idea of license and fantasy. No doubt,
like Asian masks, the Porta Pia mask, and those which adorn the breastplate
and helm of the Medici dukes, could be intended as apotropaic, designed to
deter that which they resemble—that is, to ward off evil beings. It is surely
significant that the long ears so frequently found in Michelangelo's masks
are also a feature of the devils in his *Last Judgment*. The mask of *Night* in
the New Sacristy obviously has much in common with the much later Porta
Pia mask, and perhaps it also recalls the gap-toothed satyr's head that the
young sculptor worked on in the Medici sculpture garden.[67] We are surely
confronted by lower forms of life, beings without soul and with little mind
but possessed of power. The mask beside *Sleep* in the New Sacristy and the
simplified masks in the frieze are also hollow. Perhaps the best explanation
for this is that the mind is absent in sleep, as it is in death.[68] It is hardly

FIG 29

28 Giuseppe Cesari, known as
    Cavalier d'Arpino
    Grotesque mask ca. 1595–96

    Collection of Robert Loper,
    New York

29 Michelangelo Buonarotti
    **Mask, together with uncarved
    pelt, detail of the** *Allegory of
    Night* 1526–31, abandoned,
    unfinished, in 1534

    The New Sacristy, San Lorenzo,
    Florence

30 Frans Huys, after a design by
Cornelis Floris
Mask with Snakes 1555

Rijksmuseum, Amsterdam

necessary to add that the grotesque is here no longer light entertainment: there is nothing slight or delightful or whimsical about Michelangelo's ornament, which fact makes it so surprising that it once kept company with stucco work by Giovanni da Udine.

Masks by Bronzino and Other Artists

The idea of the evacuated mask is adopted in one of the astonishing and horrible designs for masks made by Cornelis Floris (1514–1575) at an unknown date but before 1555, when they were published by Hans Liefrinck in Antwerp. In this case the eye sockets are penetrated by serpents, a motif found earlier in the representations of animal skulls in Corinthian capitals designed by the Lombardi in Venice, and the flesh has something of the character of a deflated balloon.[69] This mask bears a slight resemblance to FIG 30 one that is carved out of purple stone between the scrolling supports of the tabletop in the portrait of a young man by Agnolo Bronzino (1503–1572) in the Metropolitan Museum of Art, New York, except that in this case the skin or membrane is replaced by something that is reminiscent of the damp cloth with which sculptors cover models to inhibit drying of the clay.[70] FIGS 31, 32 There is a suggestion here of some veiled horror but also a possibility that the crumpled cloth has accidentally formed itself into a mask—as seems to have happened to the cloth around the young man's codpiece.[71] There is also a mask carved in the arm of the walnut chair, which is compact and rotund for the fingers of the sitter, should he choose to be seated. It has a FIG 33 snub face and both the ears and the horns of the masks that Michelangelo gave to the Doric columns in the vestibule of the Laurentian Library (see fig. 25) and also resembles one of the heads in Cesare da Sesto's sketchbook (see fig. 11). The idea of supplying a portrait with supplementary hybrid masks was surely a response to the effigies of the Medici dukes in the New Sacristy.

A new development can be noted in Rome about a decade after Bronzino made this portrait. Around 1547 Pellegrino Tibaldi (1527–1596) joined the artists who were working on frescoes of the life of Alexander the Great in the Sala Paolina of Castel Sant'Angelo.[72] Four drawings by him survive for masks in the decorative scheme in this room[73]—fictive bronze heads, some FIG 34 of them about the same size as the drawings, above fictive bronze reliefs.[74] FIGS 35, 36 The expressions of the masks resemble those in the narratives—something

31 Agnolo Bronzino
*Portrait of an Unknown Young
Man* 1530s

The Metropolitan Museum of
Art, New York

32 Agnolo Bronzino
Portrait of an Unknown Young Man

Detail of fig. 31

33 Agnolo Bronzino
Portrait of an Unknown Young Man

Detail of fig. 31

34   Pellegrino Tibaldi
**Four masks, probably preparatory for
frescoes in the Sala Paolina, Castel
Sant'Angelo, Rome** ca. 1547

The Morgan Library & Museum,
New York

35 Pellegrino Tibaldi
Fictive bronze relief of Alexander
burying Homer's *Iliad* in a casket,
with paler fictive bronze elements
including grotesque masks above and
below ca. 1547–48

Sala Paolina, Castel Sant'Angelo, Rome

36 Pellegrino Tibaldi with Perino del Vaga
Fictive bronze tondo relief of the
Martyrdom of Saint Paul with
grotesque mask above ca. 1547–48

Sala Paolina, Castel Sant'Angelo, Rome

that was perhaps unprecedented—and one of them is even reminiscent of
the agony of the *Laocoön*. In the three other cases, we are reminded of the
theories about the relationship between man and animal, in both facial
type and expression, which can be found in Leonardo's notebooks and in
Giambattista della Porta's treatise. It is unlikely that Tibaldi intended such
interpretations, and it is hard to find any work of art in which masks possess a clear meaning, but exceptions can be found in an inconspicuous part
of the celebrated gallery in the Palazzo Farnese that was decorated by Annibale Carracci and his associates.

At the hinges of the scallop shells within the fictive sculptural framework of the Palazzo Farnese ceiling frescoes (by Annibale Carracci [1560–
1609] or an associate) we can detect a variety of tiny grotesque heads, from
the mouths or mustaches of which festoons are suspended. The fore-
shortened fluted bivalve is thus converted into something resembling a bat
in flight.[75] This is perhaps no more than a witty form of marginal ornamental metamorphosis, but the fully colored heads elsewhere, partially
concealed from view by the cornice, have truly expressive features that are

FIGS 37, 38

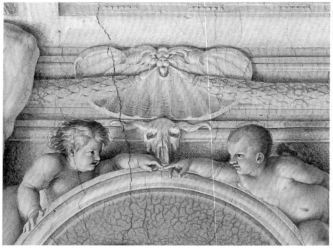

37 Annibale Carracci
Jove and Juno, including framework of
fictive stone carving featuring shell and
swags 1597–1600

Ceiling, Gallery, Palazzo Farnese, Rome

38 Annibale Carracci or associate
Fictive stone carving of shell and
swags 1597–1600

Ceiling, Gallery, Palazzo Farnese,
Rome

illustrative of agonized exclusion, festering resentment, or lewd merriment
such as serve to render the conduct of the gods elevated by comparison.[76]   FIGS 39-41
They may remind us of the masks designed by the Cavalier d'Arpino only
a couple of years earlier, but what is unusual here is the way that the faces
seem to react to the amorous activities depicted in the fictive bronze reliefs
above them.

The Auricular Cartouche and the Mask Spout

There are numerous grotesque masks in Roman painting and sculpture of
the seventeenth and eighteenth centuries, but it was in Florence that the
mask, specifically in its Michelangelesque forms, enjoyed the most vigor-
ous life for more than a century after the great sculptor's death. Such a
mask can be found on the cuirass of at least one grand duke.[77] It was also
a common means of dramatizing apertures such as keyholes and, most

40 Annibale Carracci or associate
**Masks below fictive bronze
tondo reliefs** 1597–1600

Ceiling, Gallery, Palazzo Farnese,
Rome

41 Annibale Carracci or associate
**Masks below fictive bronze
tondo reliefs** 1597–1600

Ceiling, Gallery, Palazzo Farnese,
Rome

44

42 Designed by Bernardo
Buontalenti
**Fountain spout and
basin** ca. 1574

Angular junction of Borgo San
Jacopo and Via dello Sprone,
facing Piazza de' Frescobaldi,
Florence

conspicuously, spouts, not only within grottoes but in prominent public
fountains such as the one designed by Bernardo Buontalenti (1536–1608).[78] FIG 42
And it was in Florence that the grotesque mask came to be most closely
associated with, and often deliberately concealed within, the cartouche.

As can be seen from the drawing for a pilaster panel of the early sixteenth century that was discussed above (see fig. 9), designs for ornament
were often only fully elaborated on one side of a central line because they
could be copied exactly, in reverse, by transfer to the other side. The convention arose of completing the design on the other side of the central
line with an alternative idea: a convention illustrated by a drawing made
by Fabrizio Boschi (1572–1642) in Florence, probably in the second decade
of the seventeenth century.[79] At the top of the sheet there is a mask with a FIG 43
large curling horn on one side and a smaller, inward-curling horn on the
other. Lower down, we can choose between a horned foliate mask on one
side and a curling horn or shell with a mask nestled beneath it on the other.

43 Fabrizio Boschi
Study for a Cartouche with Putti, a
Dolphin, and Masks ca. 1610–20

The Morgan Library & Museum,
New York

A fish seems to be consuming the horn, or shell, its wriggling tail supported by a nude boy.

The cartouche can be defined as a fleshy, scrolling frame. It depends on the idea of the pelt of an animal, which was then of course a common sight—as was curling parchment. In the magnificent picture frames devised for the Medici collection in the seventeenth century, the scrolls retain this organic quality, and masks can be found, more or less concealed, at the centers and corners.[80] It has been suggested that this tendency in Florentine ornament may have been given a stimulus by the auricular designs made in northern Europe in the early seventeenth century, most notably those by Adam van Vianen for silver, although there are in fact numerous earlier examples of such fleshy and gristly fantasies.[81] And it may even be relevant to observe that the mask beside Michelangelo's *Allegory of Night* seems to be attached to a pelt (see fig. 29), thus recalling the evacuated skin of Saint Bartholomew in his fresco *The Last Judgment.*

Grotesque masks continued to appeal to major European painters and sculptors in the eighteenth century. Giambattista Tiepolo, for example, was especially partial to vases with mask handles. Edmé Bouchardon (1698– 1762), who was careful to study spouts and vases in and around Rome, designed a grotesque fish mask for the bronze spouts of his great fountain in the Rue de Grenelle in Paris.[82] Grotesque masks are also often incorporated into French ormolu mounts. Jean-Charles Delafosse (1734–1789), one of the chief proponents of *le goût grec*, was especially attached to them.[83] It is curious, though, that in the final decades of the eighteenth century, when there was an intensified awareness of Roman mural painting,[84] so much more of which was then being uncovered in the vicinity of Naples, and a great revival of interest in Giovanni da Udine,[85] much that we would call grotesque in common modern usage—the weird hybrid, the wriggling monster, the ugly or screaming mask—was excluded from the numerous new, elegant imitations of grotesque ornament.

FIG 44

FIG 45

FIG 46

Revivals

With the revival of medieval styles in the mid-nineteenth century, the Green Man mask reappeared, freely interpreted, in capitals, corbels, and keystones, which are especially rampant on some of the brownstone town houses of New York.[86] At the same time, sixteenth-century Italian ornament

44 Edmé Bouchardon
**Fountain spout designed
ca. 1575 by Giacomo della
Porta** ca. 1723–26

The Morgan Library & Museum,
New York

45 **Bronze spout, cast from a model made by Edmé Bouchardon** ca. 1741

Fontaine des Quatre-Saisons, Rue de Grenelle, Paris

46 Jean-Charles Delafosse
Design probably for ormolu ca. 1760–70

The Morgan Library & Museum, New York

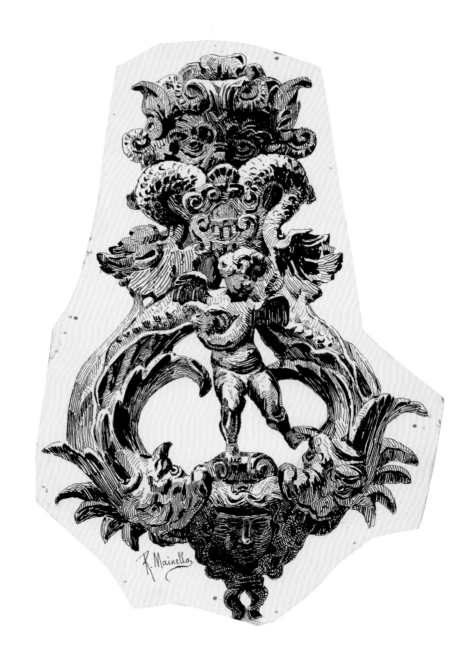

began to be imitated. Benvenuto Cellini, who loved all that was weird and wriggling and screaming in the grotesque, enjoyed a new popularity. Artists such as Raffaelle Mainella (1856–1941), a highly successful watercolorist who was also in demand as an interior decorator, studied the metalwork of sixteenth-century Venice.[87] This was the age of museum collecting and of the reproduction of ornament, but genuine invention can be found more frequently than is commonly supposed in the ornamental architecture and architectural ornament of New York in the early twentieth century. Only a block away from the Morgan Library, where Thirty-Seventh Street meets Fifth Avenue, a building is clad to the point of congestion with terracotta enrichments, including masks of several sizes and supporting satyrs, that might have been inspired by Clovio's borders—with a topical addition to indicate the hatting business conducted within.[88]

FIG 47

FIGS 48, 49

More orthodox and certainly more elegant examples of "cinquecento taste" are the bronze flagpole stands designed in 1910 by Thomas Hastings (1860–1929) of the architectural firm of Hastings and Carrère, which were erected in 1911 outside the New York Public Library. These were modeled by Raffaelle Menconi, who may have helped to devise the details, perhaps adding the masks of four different racial types.[89] The mustaches and pigtails of the Chinese match aspects of grotesque masks of the sixteenth century, and the feather headdress of the Native American resembles the architectural diadems that so commonly crown them. Since the nude seated figures, male and female, on the stands represent Adventure, Discovery, Conquest, and Civilization, we might assume that these masks are intended to represent inferior and subject races, but there is in fact also a Caucasian face, so presumably they simply represent humanity in all its variety.[90]

FIGS 50–54

The nearly complete severance of sculpture from architecture that occurred roughly a hundred years ago marks a decisive change in European art. Great sculptors thereafter have seldom been interested in ornament. With painting, the story is different. Italian craftsmen re-created famous Renaissance ceilings for Mr. Morgan's library. Lodovico Pogliaghi

48 Detail of terracotta ornament
    on the Thirty-Seventh Street
    facade of No. 411, Fifth
    Avenue ca. 1915

49 Detail of terracotta ornament
    on the Thirty-Seventh Street
    facade of No. 411, Fifth
    Avenue ca. 1915

(1857–1950) created, with astonishing skill, work in the style of Giovanni da Udine in the Villa Carlotta by the banks of Lake Como.[91] However, Pogliaghi, esteemed in his day as a painter, sculptor, and stage designer, has been largely forgotten.[92] Our idea of what a great artist should do was established in nineteenth-century France. We know that the young Édouard Manet drew some of the figures in the grotesque decorations by Alessandro Allori on the vaults of the Uffizi corridors,[93] but he would never have considered the creation of ornament to be a worthy occupation for a serious artist. Indeed, few prominent painters in the last 150 years have designed ornament. And yet the urge to create polymorphic monsters and curious hybrids, when denied one outlet, found another and became, in the work of

50 Designed by Thomas Hastings
**Base of a bronze flagstaff (one of a
pair)** 1910

New York Public Library, New York

such artists as Paul Klee, Joan Miró, and many of the Surrealists, a favorite
subject for easel paintings. In such work, the deliberately enigmatic, the
witty improvisation, the meaningful nonsense, and the terrifying monster
may be said to have invaded the painting from their previous home in the
margin and the frame.

51 Designed by Thomas Hastings
Base of a bronze flagstaff (one of a pair)

Detail of fig. 50, showing Native American face

52 Designed by Thomas Hastings
Base of a bronze flagstaff (one of a pair)

Detail of fig. 50, showing Chinese face

53 Designed by Thomas Hastings
Base of a bronze flagstaff (one of a pair)

Detail of fig. 50, showing African face

54 Designed by Thomas Hastings
Base of a bronze flagstaff (one of a pair)

Detail of fig. 50, showing Caucasian face

Notes

I would like to express my gratitude to Colin Bailey for welcoming me to the Morgan Library & Museum, and to John Marciari for the invitation to work in the Drawing Institute as Thaw Senior Fellow. John Marciari, Zoe Watnik, Joshua O'Driscoll, and Alexandra Coutavas attended to my every scholarly need. And the friendly assistance provided by staff at the Morgan, as also in the Print Room and the Watson Library in the Metropolitan Museum of Art, made my stay in New York especially fruitful. I would also like to thank the following for help with different aspects of my research: Adriano Aymonimo, Elizabeth Bernick, Marco Bolzoni, Giada Damen, Caroline Elam, James Fenton, Kristen Hudson, Alison Luchs, Louise Rice, Xavier Salomon, Luke Syson, Jennifer Tonkovich, and Kathleen Weil Garris-Brandt. As always, my text has been greatly improved by Mary Crettier.

1 There are two major modern commentaries on the *Farnese Hours*, one by Webster Smith, which accompanies the first facsimile edition (undated but published in New York in 1976), and the other by William M. Voelkle for the second facsimile edition, published in Graz in 2001, in which there is also a full account of Clovio's life and art by Ivan Golub.

2 Figure 1: Fols. 17v–18r; tempera with gold on vellum; each leaf 173 × 109 mm; The Morgan Library & Museum, New York, inv. MS M.69. Vasari, who in his life of Clovio describes every major illustration in the *Hours*, identifies this frame as "l'ornamento finto di metallo." It might now be mistaken for walnut, but in the Renaissance bronze seems to have been more familiar in its unpatinated color. *Le vite de' più eccelenti pittori e scultori e architettori nelle redazioni del 1500 e 1568*, ed. Rosanna Bettarini and Paola Barocchi, 6 vols. (Rome, 1966–87), 6 (1987): 215. Vasari uses "ornamento," "fregio

ornato," and "fregiature" to describe the frames.

3 Figure 2: Fol. 30v; tempera with gold on vellum, 173 × 109 mm; The Morgan Library & Museum, New York, inv. MS M.69.

4 Figure 3: Fols. 63v–64r; tempera with gold on vellum, 173 × 109 mm; The Morgan Library & Museum, New York, inv. MS M.69.

5 For Smith "presumably," but for Voelkle "undoubtedly," these nudes are references to Bathsheba, though they could not of course be representations of her.

6 The mask on the right has wings, so perhaps references to the elements of air and water were intended—although, if so, why?

7 The history of the "beautiful" female mask is not explored here. It was especially popular on Venetian keystones in the sixteenth century, and thereafter very common in furniture and metalwork throughout Europe, where a radiant Apollonian head is also often found.

8 For Giovanni da Udine's work there, see Nicole Dacos and Caterina Furlan, *Giovanni da Udine, 1487–1561*, 3 vols. (Udine, 1987), 1:61–93; also Nicole Dacos, *The Loggia of Raphael: A Vatican Art Treasure* (New York, 2008).

9 Figure 7: Fresco; The Vatican Palace, Vatican City. For the Domus Aurea and its rediscovery, see above all Paul G. P. Meyboom and Eric M. Moormann, *Le decorazioni dipinte e marmoree della domus aurea di Nerone a Roma*, 2 vols. (Leuven, 2013). Also Nicole Dacos, *La découverte de la Domus Aurea et la formation des grotesques à la Renaissance* (London, 1969).

10 The ornament in the Piccolomini Library, Siena Cathedral, was described as that "che hoggi chiamano grottesche" in the contract with Pinturicchio of June 1502. Juergen Schulz, "Pinturicchio and the Revival of Antiquity,"

Journal of the Warburg and Courtauld Institutes 25 (1962): 47.

11 Peter Meller, "Manet in Italy: Some Newly Identified Sources for His Early Sketchbooks," *Burlington Magazine* 144 (February 2002): 68–110, at 82. The best succinct account of this type of ornament is provided by Peter Ward-Jackson, *Some Main Streams and Tributaries in European Ornament from 1500 to 1750* (London, 1969; reprinted 1972), a classic text now not easily obtained (first published as three essays in the *Victoria and Albert Museum Bulletin* in 1967). A comprehensive account has been supplied by Alessandra Zamperini, *Le grottesche: Il sogno della pittura nella decorazione parietale* (San Giovanni Lupatoto, 2007).

12 Vitruvius, *De architectura* 7.5.3–4; and Horace, *De arte poetica* 8–11.

13 Already in 1522 he addresses a letter from Venice to "Charissimo mio patrone et magior onorando Michelangelo." Elio Bartolini, *Giovanni da Udine: La vita* (Udine, 1987), 57.

14 See Caterina Furlan, in Dacos and Furlan, *Giovanni da Udine*, 1:54–59, and Alessandro Cecchi, "Le perdute decorazioni fiorentine di Giovanni da Udine," *Paragone* 34, no. 399 (May 1983): 20–41. See also William E. Wallace, *Michelangelo at San Lorenzo* (Cambridge, 1994) for relevant contracts and evidence.

15 Vasari himself suggested to Cosimo I that he would like to extend the grotesque ornament. See Karl Frey, ed., *Der literarische Nachlass Giorgio Vasaris* (Munich, 1923), 719–80. For Vasari's description of the work and the "fogliami, ucelli [sic], maschere e figure" see *Le vite*, 5 (1984): 454. For the date of its destruction, see Cecchi, "Le perdute decorazioni fiorentine di Giovanni da Udine," 39–40 n. 46.

16 Work was completed there in 1507. For Pinturicchio and antique ornament generally, see Schulz, "Pinturicchio and the Revival of Antiquity."

17 For Bimbo, see especially Alessandro Cecchi, *The Piccolomini Library in the Cathedral of Siena* (Florence, 1982), 15.

18 Figure 8: Tin-glazed earthenware; private collection.

19 The majority of these tiles are in the Victoria and Albert Museum, London (where there is one with the date of 1509), and in the Musée du Louvre, Paris. For the equivalents in the Domus Aurea, see Meyboom and Moormann, *Le decorazione*, 1:240–41, 2:188.

20 Figure 9: Pen and brown ink over black chalk, 281 × 207 mm; The Morgan Library & Museum, New York, inv. 1981.85.

21 Max Lehrs, *Martin Schongauer: The Complete Engravings; A Catalogue Raisonné*, rev. ed. (San Francisco, 2005), 208–11. He notes (209–10) that the nine monsters are all based on parts of actual creatures ranging from dragonflies to tuna fish and an antelope skull.

22 Figure 10: Egg tempera on panel, 47 × 35 cm; Kimbell Art Museum, Fort Worth, inv. AP 2009.01. The painting may just possibly be by another pupil of Ghirlandaio, since he is unlikely to have devised this exercise (prompted by recognition of his own deficient "fantasia") for one pupil alone, but, even if not by the young Michelangelo, it gives a good idea of what Michelangelo's work would have looked like.

23 Elizabeth Bernick will publish a full account of these drawings, tracing the artist's sources and demonstrating that they do indeed come from some sort of sketchbook. I am grateful to her for looking at them with me and sharing her discoveries.

24 Figure 11: Pen and brown ink, 191 × 141 mm; The Morgan Library & Museum, New York, inv. II, 34. The crab claws must have been suggested by an antique mask of Oceanus, and perhaps specifically by the Bocca della Verità, where they are now hardly legible. See Fabio Barry, "The Mouth of Truth and the Forum Boarium: Oceanus, Hercules, and Hadrian," *Art Bulletin* 93 (2011): 7–37. The theme was taken up and developed in one of the most bizarre of Cornelis Floris's engraved masks based on lobsters rather than a crab. Crabs also feature in Giuliano da Sangallo's sketchbook (Biblioteca Comunale degli Intronati, Siena).

25 Figure 12: Pen and brown ink over black and red chalk, 187 × 141 mm; The Morgan Library & Museum, New York, inv. II, 48.

26 Figure 13: Fol. 1; tempera and gilding on vellum, 810 × 560 mm; The Morgan Library & Museum, New York, inv. MS M.912.

27 Figure 14: Bronze, 9.5 × 22.2 × 15.2 cm; The Metropolitan Museum of Art, New York, Gift of Ogden Mills, inv. 25.142.7. For the character of marine hybrids (which are foliate not only on the face), see the numerous examples in Alison Luchs, *The Mermaids of Venice* (Turnhout, 2010). For masks of Oceanus in the Golden

House, see Meyboom and Moormann, *Le deco-razione*, 1:224–25, 2:149, and 1:158–59, 2:35.

28 The Green Man has excited much ardent amateur scholarship (see, for example, Julia Hamilton Somerset, Lady Raglan, "The 'Green Man' in Church Architecture," *Folklore* 50 [March 1939]: 45–57). The term "foliate mask" is preferred in most modern surveys of ornament (for example, Philippa Lewis and Gillian Darley, *Dictionary of Ornament* [London, 1986]).

29 Those by Enea Vico were especially influential. See, for example, the "rinceau with mask and sea monsters" (conveniently illustrated in Janet Byrne, *Renaissance Ornament Prints and Drawings* [New York, 1981], 15).

30 An example is the mask in the frieze of the Chapel of the Assumption in San Cristoforo, Vercelli, by Gaudenzio Ferrari, reproduced in Julian-Matthias Kliemann and Michael Rohlmann, *Italian Frescoes: High Renaissance and Mannerism, 1500–1610* (Munich, 2004), 321, fig. 139.

31 Figure 15: Pen and brown ink, 183 × 186 mm; The British Museum, London, inv. 1895-9-15-496 verso. Figure 16: Carved wood with water gilding over gesso; Gallerie degli Uffizi, Florence, inv. 1890 no. 1456.

32 It is not unusual for an artist to turn a sheet; nevertheless, it is striking that Michelangelo was interested in turning masks upside down, for that is how the bearded mask is held by the putto in a strange allegorical drawing, which is known only in a copy by Battista Franco in the Gallerie degli Uffizi, Florence (inv. 614E).

33 This observation was made verbally.

34 Figure 17: Carrara marble; The New Sacristy, San Lorenzo, Florence.

35 Howard Burns, in *Andrea Palladio: The Portico and the Farmyard*, exh. cat., London: Hayward Gallery, 1975, 267–68, nos. 496–97 (I owe this reference to Caroline Elam).

36 Figure 18: Carrara marble; The New Sacristy, San Lorenzo, Florence. It is somehow reminiscent of the beak-head ornament found in northern European Romanesque architecture, which Michelangelo cannot have known. There is considerable variation in the quality of execution, and probably also in the interpretation of Michelangelo's design by the carvers. Michelangelo's preference for and confidence in Silvio Cosini was clearly expressed in 1524. See Marco Campigli, "Silvio

Cosini e Michelangelo," *Nuovi studi* 12 (2006): 93–94, 97.

37 For bust reliefs by or associated with Verrocchio (including the marble relief of Alexander in the National Gallery of Art in Washington) and taken up by Leonardo (notably in a famous drawing of a warrior in the British Museum), see the judicious discussion by Andrew Butterfield, *The Sculptures of Andrea del Verrocchio* (New Haven, 1997), 156–57, and plates 205, 207, 208. For Giuliano da Sangallo, see his sketchbook in the Biblioteca Comunale degli Intronati, especially fols. 38v, 39v, and 40. Caroline Elam drew this to my attention.

38 Figure 19: Carrara marble; The New Sacristy, San Lorenzo, Florence.

39 On this topic, see the extraordinary second paragraph of Walter Pater's essay of 1871, "The Poetry of Michelangelo," republished in *The Renaissance: Studies in Art and Poetry* (London, 1873).

40 Figure 20: Carrara marble; The New Sacristy, San Lorenzo, Florence.

41 Good terracotta examples of such from the fourth century B.C. were acquired by the Metropolitan Museum of Art in 1896 (e.g., an antefix, inv. 96.18.160), and massive stone versions are a prominent feature of the museum's facade.

42 The one to the right as we face the altar; the other was recarved much later.

43 Campigli, "Silvio Cosini e Michelangelo," 85–116.

44 Figure 21: Carrara marble; The Metropolitan Museum of Art, New York, inv. 58.121. The doorway, which arrived in the museum in forty-three pieces, had previously adorned the New York residence of Charles T. Barney. It was sold to the museum by Mitchell Samuels of French & Co. in 1958 and seems (from notes in the departmental file) to have been considered by the curators as perhaps Spanish, which explains its location in the Blumenthal Patio, otherwise decorated with architectural elements from the castle of Vélez Blanco in Andalusia, Spain.

45 Figure 22: Black chalk, 39 × 137 mm; The Morgan Library & Museum, New York, inv. II, 32a. Formerly bound with sheets from the Cesare da Sesto sketchbook. The drawing has been proposed as perhaps the work of Camillo Boccaccino, but I was unable to discover who made this suggestion or why. For the monsters in the New Sacristy and especially those on

the candelabra, see Campigli, "Silvio Cosini e Michelangelo," 102–4.

46 Figure 23: Carrara marble; Tomb of Pope Julius II, incorporated in lowest register; San Pietro in Vincoli, Rome. Figure 24: Carrara marble; Tomb of Pope Julius II, San Pietro in Vincoli, Rome. The ornamental elements seem mostly to have been executed in 1513–14 by Antonio da Pontassieve (Claudia Echinger Maurach, in Christoph Frommel, *Michelangelo's Tomb of Pope Julius II: Genesis and Genius* [Milan, 2014], 285, and see also doc. 57, 309). But the style of fig. 24 here must be later, perhaps about 1533, soon after which date the lower stage of the monument was assembled.

47 Michelangelo did take some interest in the technique of working in stucco, as is clear from a letter to Giovanni da Udine (Bartolini, *Giovanni da Udine*, 65).

48 The Lorenzetti relief is illustrated in Dacos and Furlan, *Giovanni da Udine*, 1:36, 43. At least some of the carved walnut panels in the fronts of the desks in the Laurentian Library, San Lorenzo, look as if they were executed after Michelangelo's designs, and stylistically this would seem to belong to a slightly earlier phase than the second of the panels discussed here.

49 C. Caneva, *I soffiti nei corridoi e nelle sale in gli Uffizi: Catalogo generale* (Florence, 1979), 1117–18.

50 His drawings of ceilings of the Domus Aurea are in the Escorial. José da Felicidade, ed., *Álbum dos desenhos das antiqualhas de Francisco de Holanda* (Lisbon, 1989), especially fols. 47–48. It is important to note that De Hollanda also knew of Roman murals in the vicinity of Naples (in Pozzuoli and Baia), which cannot now be identified. See Francisco De Hollanda, *On Antique Painting*, trans. Alice Sedgwick Wohl (University Park, PA, 2013), 148.

51 See the introductory essay by Joaquim Olivieira Caetano and the notes by Helmut Wohl in De Hollanda, *On Antique Painting*.

52 De Hollanda, *On Antique Painting*, 207–8. David Summers, *Michelangelo and the Language of Art* (Princeton, 1981), 135–37, provides an excellent commentary on this and relates it to the copy after Schongauer.

53 De Hollanda, *On Antique Painting*, 209.

54 Charles Hope, "Francisco De Hollanda and Art Theory, Humanism and Neoplatonism in Italy," in De Hollanda, *On Antique Painting*, 60, 62 n. 2.

55 The most notable of these is the design for an oil lamp in the Fogg Art Museum, Harvard University, inv. 1932.152.

56 This confusing and mysterious passage is expertly unwrapped by Summers, *Michelangelo and the Language of Art*, 256–61.

57 Summers, *Michelangelo and the Language of Art*, 26–27.

58 Thus, for example, the grotesque panels of the Julius tomb are not included in the catalogue of the sculptures in Frommel, *Michelangelo's Tomb of Pope Julius II*, 301–3.

59 For an excellent account of what was novel in the architecture of the New Sacristy, its relationship to Vitruvian ideas, and how it was interpreted by the artist's contemporaries, see Caroline Elam, "'Tuscan Dispositions': Michelangelo's Florentine Architectural Vocabulary and Its Reception," *Renaissance Studies* 19, no. 1 (2005): 46–81.

60 Figure 25: Pietra bigio; staircase vestibule, Laurentian Library, San Lorenzo, Florence. Giulio Carlo Argan and Bruno Contardi, *Michelangelo architetto* (Milan, 1990), 190.

61 For the Palazzo dei Conservatori, see Argan and Contardi, *Michelangelo architetto*, 257. Work commenced there in 1563.

62 Figure 26: Travertine; Palazzo dei Conservatori, Rome.

63 Figure 27: Travertine; Porta Pia, Rome.

64 Far smaller masks with outspread birds' wings, parodic cherubim, serve as corbels below the blind rectangular frames either side of this great arch. For a thorough account of the Porta Pia, see Golo Maurer, in *Michelangelo: Architetto a Roma*, exh. cat., Rome: Musei Capitolini, 2009, 226–39, where, however, the sculptural elements are not discussed.

65 As the final one in a series of thirty-eight etchings of masks by Aloisio Giovannoli, undated.

66 Figure 28: Black and red chalk, 210 × 190 mm; Collection of Robert Loper, New York. Marco Simone Bolzoni brought the drawing by Arpino to my attention. It is published in his "Cavalier d'Arpino: Omaggio a Michelangelo," in *Dopo il 1564: L'eredità di Michelangelo a Roma nel tardo cinquecento*, ed. Marco Simone Bolzoni, Furio Rinaldi, and Patrizia Tosini (Rome, 2016), 120–41, fig. 21. A comparable drawing in the Harvard Art Museums is fig. 22 in the same essay.

67 Figure 29: Carrara marble; The New Sacristy, San Lorenzo, Florence.

68 In the case of the mask beside *Sleep*, there is a creature within but at some distance from the exterior of the mask.

69 Figure 30: Engraving, 158 × 143 mm; Rijksmuseum, Amsterdam, inv. RP-P-1888-A-12651.

70 Figure 31: Oil on panel, 95.6 × 74.9 cm; The Metropolitan Museum of Art, New York, H. O. Havemeyer Collection, Bequest of Mrs. H. O. Havemeyer, 1929, inv. 29.100.16.

71 This could in fact just possibly be an accidental effect. It is not known when or by whom it was first pointed out in print, but it is now mentioned on the museum's website in a catalogue text credited to Andrea Bayer.

72 A succinct account of the Sala Paolina is provided by Kliemann and Rohlmann, *Italian Frescoes*, 352–57.

73 Figure 34: Pen and brown ink with brown wash with white opaque watercolor, over black chalk on discolored blue paper, 211 × 173 mm; The Morgan Library & Museum, New York, inv. 1979.9.

74 Figure 35: Fresco; Sala Paolina, Castel Sant'Angelo, Rome. Figure 36: Fresco; Sala Paolina, Castel Sant'Angelo, Rome.

75 Figure 37: Fresco; ceiling of Gallery, Palazzo Farnese, Rome. Figure 38: Fresco; ceiling of Gallery, Palazzo Farnese, Rome.

76 Figure 39: Fresco; ceiling of Gallery, Palazzo Farnese, Rome. Figure 40: Fresco; ceiling of Gallery, Palazzo Farnese, Rome. Figure 41: Fresco; ceiling of Gallery, Palazzo Farnese, Rome.

77 This is the bust with a porphyry head of Ferdinand II de' Medici (created grand duke in 1621, so executed soon after that date) in the Antiricetto of the Gallerie degli Uffizi (inv. 1914 no. 45). The carving of the mask as well as of the ruff is of the utmost virtuosity.

78 Figure 42: Carrara marble; junction of Borgo San Jacopo and Via dello Sprone, facing Piazza de' Frescobaldi, Florence. For a superb gilt bronze keyhole escutcheon, see the Fitzwilliam Coin Cabinet, Ashmolean Museum, Oxford. For Buontalenti, see Ida Maria Botto, in *Dizionario biografico italiano* (Rome, 1972), 15: s.v. "Buontalenti, Bernardo."

79 Figure 43: Red chalk, 191 × 165 mm; The Morgan Library & Museum, New York, Gift of Kate Ganz, inv. 1992.1. I have not been able

to discover who recognized this as a work by Boschi. The attribution had been made before the drawing was donated to the Morgan Library.

80 For frames of this kind, see Marilena Mosco, *Cornici dei Medici: La fantasia barocca al servizio del potere* (Florence, 2007).

81 Ward-Jackson, *Some Main Streams and Tributaries in European Ornament*, 39–41.

82 Figure 44: Pen and brown ink and black chalk on two sheets pasted onto one page, 187 × 131 mm; The Morgan Library & Museum, New York, inv. 2006.16:1. Bouchardon's drawing (perhaps traced) is of the fountain spout designed ca. 1575 by Giacomo della Porta, formerly on the Fontana del Moro in Piazza Navona, Rome (now Museo Pietro Canonica, Rome), together with a study of a grotesque winged mask in travertine probably of the seventeenth century on the corner of a house in Via dei Redentoristi, Rome. Figure 45: Bronze; Fontaine des Quatre-Saisons, Rue de Grenelle, Paris. The bronze spout is one of a pair, cast from a model made by Bouchardon, ca. 1741, for the Fontaine des Quatre-Saisons in the Rue de Grenelle, Paris (completed 1745). See also the vestiges of auricular forms in Bouchardon's fountain design in the Metropolitan Museum of Art (inv. 1978.27), published in Mary L. Myers, *French Architectural and Ornament Drawings of the Eighteenth Century*, exh. cat., New York: Metropolitan Museum of Art, 1991, 30–31, no. 18. For Bouchardon's Roman studies, see Anne-Lise Desmas, "Edmé Bouchardon's *Vade Mecum* in Rome: Sketchbooks in the Morgan Library & Museum," *Master Drawings* 56, no. 1 (Spring 2018): 31–84 (for the page illustrated here, see 33, 49).

83 Figure 46: Pen and ink, 422 × 212 mm; The Morgan Library & Museum, New York, inv. 1966.10:44. This example is fol. 26 in an album of late eighteenth-century designs for interior decor and decorative arts formerly belonging to Wyatt Papworth (1822–1894). For Delafosse, a sculptor by training and an architect by aspiration, see Myers, *French Architectural and Ornament Drawings*, 53–63. A drawing of a ewer in the Metropolitan Museum of Art (inv. 80.3.664; Myers, 57, no. 32) is close to the drawing in the Morgan reproduced here and perhaps prompted the attribution of the latter by Elaine Evans Dee to Delafosse.

84 Meyboom and Moormann, *Le decorazione*, 6–10, provides a valuable account of the later interest in the Domus Aurea.

85 Giovanni Volpato's prints of the Loggia of Leo X, published between 1772 and 1777, are an example of the interest in the eighteenth century in Giovanni da Udine, as is the near replica of the Loggia erected in the Winter Palace in Saint Petersburg by Giacomo Quarenghi in the following decade (1778–88).

86 The greatest concentration is on West Eighty-First Street.

87 Figure 47: Pen and ink, 121 × 85 mm; The Morgan Library & Museum, New York, inv. 2006.45:47. The drawing by Mainella illustrated here comes from an album with a cover in Japanese taste, compiled about 1890, titled "Miscellanea: Disegni a penna di artisti Veneziani." Other drawings therein are signed by Giacomo Favretto (1849–1878), Ettore Tito (1859–1941), and Pietro Fragiacomo (1856–1922).

88 Figure 48: Terracotta; Thirty-Seventh Street facade, 411 Fifth Avenue, New York. Figure 49: Terracotta; Thirty-Seventh Street facade, 411 Fifth Avenue, New York. The architects of this building were Warren and Wetmore, but the designer of the ornament, executed by New York Architectural Terracotta, is not known. Hatmakers were noted as being among the first occupants of the building, and one old firm (Bollman) still uses the building. Zoe Watnik alerted me to the research conducted on this building by Tom Miller, "Daytonian in Manhattan" (blog), September 6, 2012.

89 Figure 50: Bronze; New York Public Library, 476 Fifth Avenue, New York, cast by the Tiffany Foundry and erected in front of the New York Public Library in 1911. The attribution to Hastings is confirmed by drawings in the New York Public Library. A photograph of the plaster model (New York Public Library, inv. Arc. R G10 5928, from the Henry Hope Reed Collection) is endorsed with the name of Menconi as the modeler and credits a certain Grandelli with the modeling of the figures.

90 Sodoma had incorporated allusions to the four corners of the Earth in the grotesques he painted on the pilasters of the cloisters at Monte Oliveto Maggiore, 1505–8, but otherwise, surprisingly, I have found no precedents for this theme. For the depiction of racial types in North American sculpture around 1900, see the *Four Continents* by Daniel Chester French for the New York Customs House.

91 His model was the work by Giovanni da Udine in Villa Madama, which had been carefully restored not long before.

92 For Poliaghi, see Paola Bosio, in *Dizionario degli italiani* (Rome, 2015), 84: s.v. "Poliaghi, Lodovico." Work at the Villa Carlotta on Lake Como was undertaken for Georg II of Saxe-Meiningen and his wife, Carlotta, daughter of Albert of Prussia, between 1905 and 1910. The entrance vestibule and the Sala delle Vedute are especially noteworthy.

93 Meller, "Manet in Italy" (see n. 11 above).

The
Morgan
Drawing
Institute

This is a publication of a lecture delivered on
June 12, 2018, at the Morgan Library & Museum.
The lecture and publication are programs of
the Morgan Drawing Institute.

LIBRARY OF CONGRESS CATALOGING-IN-
PUBLICATION DATA
Names: Penny, Nicholas, 1949– author.
Title: The zoomorphic mask / Nicholas Penny.
Description: New York : Drawing Institute,
    The Morgan Library & Museum, [2019] | "The
    Annual Thaw Lecture 2018, Drawing Institute." |
    Includes bibliographical references.
Identifiers: LCCN 2019004958 |
    ISBN 9780875981932 (pbk. : alk. paper)
Subjects: LCSH: Masks in art. | Fantastic, The,
    in art. | Decoration and ornament, Renaissance.
Classification: LCC N8222.M39 P46 2019 |
    DDC 709.02/4—dc23
LC record available at https://lccn.loc.gov
    /2019004958

Published by the Morgan Library & Museum,
New York
    themorgan.org

Produced by Lucia|Marquand, Seattle
    luciamarquand.com

Series design by Jeff Wincapaw
Layout by Meghann Ney
Typeset in Calluna and Whitney by
    Brynn Warriner
Copyedited by Fronia W. Simpson
Proofread by Laura Lesswing
Color management by iocolor, Seattle
Printed and bound in China by C&C Offset
    Printing Co., Ltd.

Front and back cover: Detail of fig. 34
Page 2: Detail of fig. 34
Page 4: Detail of fig. 2
Page 8: Detail of fig. 28
Page 56: Detail of fig. 43